Being Irish . . .

D1594623

Being Irish . . .

Contemplations on the Nature and Meaning of the Irish Race

Joe Keefe

Andrews McMeel Publishing

Kansas City

Being Irish . . .

02 03 04 05 06 BIN 10 9 8 7 6 5 4 3 2 1

ISBN: 0-7407-1997-1

Library of Congress Control Number: 2001088022

Check out Joe Keefe's Web site at
www.Humor-Resources.com
for all your humor needs!

These wiseass remarks are dedicated with much
love to Mom and Dad,
and I couldn't do anything without Karen.

Introduction

This book lovingly shares the nature and meaning of being part of the Irish race; which is in itself ironic because very few Irish people race anywhere. The Irish are legendary among nationalities for their wit, love of life, and overwhelming propensity to procreate. In fact, the rest of the world has said to the Irish many times, "Hey cool it, will ya?"

Growing up Irish is mostly a blast. The Irish don't take themselves too seriously (of course, no one else does either), and we don't take life too seriously as well. As the old saying goes "You're only visiting here . . ." so we might as well have some fun while we're at it.

The Irish are a people filled with joy, wit, love, beer, and more beer; there is always a song in their hearts even if they don't know the words. The Irish have an odd habit of alternating between hugging and fistfighting, but nobody can hit very hard anyway so it all seems to work out.

Being born Irish signals to the world that you have a bright future as a petty criminal, politician, lawyer, carpenter, clog dancer, or barkeep—and many Irishpersons combine all of these occupations into one glorious career. Note, we are an incredibly horny race so be careful at last call.

Virtually every person in the world is "part Irish," and on at least one day each year, the world celebrates its greenness. The next day, the world celebrates the invention of aspirin.

The "jokes" contained in this book are intended as "comedy" and/or "humor." No offense is meant to any person, place, thing, or bakery item. Having said this, some persons of a delicate nature may still be slightly offended by the gentle nudgings in this book. To those people, I say *pogue mahon*.

Disclaimer: The "jokes" contained herein may be slightly offensive to persons of non-Irish descent, Druids, and people with "good taste"—while these categories are admittedly quite small, our lawyers tell us to warn you anyway. Please note that if you do take offense . . . we will provide the illusion that we care.

Being Irish means . . .

you will never play
professional basketball.

Being Irish means . . .

you have a two-beer limit . . .
for foreplay.

Being Irish means . . .

you swear very well.

Being Irish means . . .

at least one of your cousins
holds political office.

Being Irish means . . .

you don't have to change
mayors a lot.

Being Irish means . . .

you have been bribed
or you have bribed someone
or you will soon.

Being Irish means . . .

you *think* you sing very well.

Being Irish means . . .

you have no idea
how to make a long story short.

Being Irish means . . .

you are very good at playing
a lot of very bad golf.

Being Irish means . . .

you will not be able to remember
the names of all your cousins,
aunts, and uncles . . .
or brothers and sisters.

Being Irish means . . .

your parents can't
remember your name.

Being Irish means . . .

you probably need
at least nine steps of any
twelve-step program.

Being Irish means . . .

you are very good
at sneaking into a dark house . . .
and out of one, too.

Being Irish means . . .

at least two of the Ten
Commandments are optional.

Being Irish means . . .

you spent a good portion of
your childhood at a wake.

Being Irish means . . .

you're either fast or hungry.

Being Irish means . . .

there isn't a huge difference
between losing your temper
and killing someone.

Being Irish means . . .

you know how to throw up.

Being Irish means . . .

that just because you're
throwing up, doesn't mean
you aren't horny.

Being Irish means . . .

you stood in line
for most everything.

Being Irish means . . .

much of your food was boiled.

Being Irish means . . .

Mom gave up counting anything,
including children.

Being Irish means . . .

Dad never gave up on Mom.

Being Irish means . . .

your Mom got pregnant
every spring.

Being Irish means . . .

hangovers were once a hobby.

Being Irish means . . .

you have a sensitive,
caring nature . . .
when you're horny.

Being Irish means . . .

you're always horny.

Being Irish means . . .

you are Mom's favorite.

Being Irish means . . .

all your brothers and sisters
were spoiled rotten.

Being Irish means . . .

you know how to apologize,
but rarely do it.

Being Irish means . . .

your biceps are overdeveloped
from the continual lifting
of twelve ounces.

Being Irish means . . .

everyone knows your
deepest darkest secrets;
your sister already told them.

Being Irish means . . .

you guard your genitalia
before you guard your head.

Being Irish means . . .

you're surprised that no one
listens to you more.

Being Irish means . . .

you even bore *yourself* sometimes.

Being Irish means . . .

you have never hit your head
on the ceiling.

Being Irish means . . .

you have many times hit your head
on the headboard.

Being Irish means . . .

you're mad at at least one person
in your family.

Being Irish means . . .

the worst part about golf
is having to put your beer down
to shoot.

Being Irish means . . .

your coolest stuff is hidden
or it would be destroyed.

Being Irish means . . .

the bathroom is
permanently occupied.

Being Irish means . . .

you enjoy ugly clothes.

Being Irish means . . .

you either need glasses . . .
or you're crazy.

Being Irish means . . .

you have had enough potatoes
for several lives.

Being Irish means . . .

at least once, you sobered up
just in time for Mass.

Being Irish means . . .

you were smarter
than any of your teachers.

Being Irish means . . .

your teachers hit you
with some pleasure.

Being Irish means . . .

you're "finished" long before
your partner.

Being Irish means . . .

at least once, you were just
sneaking in when your parents
were just getting up.

Being Irish means . . .

at least once, the cops
let you off because of
your last name.

Being Irish means . . .

at least once, the cops
busted you because you
couldn't keep your mouth shut.

Being Irish means . . .

you have a *lot* of friends, but not
many who know the "real" you.

Being Irish means . . .

even *you* don't know
the "real" you.

Being Irish means . . .

your aunt makes the
best cookies in the world.

Being Irish means . . .

your sister doesn't.

Being Irish means . . .

someone in your family
talks too loudly.

Being Irish means . . .

someone else in your family
can't hear anything.

Being Irish means . . .

at least one person in your family
is yelling right now.

Being Irish means . . .

at sporting events, for some reason,
the people around you seem
very uncomfortable.

Being Irish means . . .

you've had food thrown at you.

Being Irish means . . .

you've caught it and eaten it.

Being Irish means . . .

you can name the disciples.

Being Irish means . . .

you know what the word
"covet" means.

Being Irish means . . .

you spent a good portion of
your childhood kneeling.

Being Irish means . . .

when you were younger,
your hair was too long,
and now you don't have
enough of it.

Being Irish means . . .

someone in your family
has red hair.

Being Irish means . . .

you have several names.

Being Irish means . . .

you shared a bedroom . . .
sometimes with a convicted felon.

Being Irish means . . .

you shared a bathroom . . .
with way too many people.

Being Irish means . . .

you're strangely poetic
after a few beers.

Being Irish means . . .

you're poetic a lot.

Being Irish means . . .

you will be punched for
no good reason . . . a lot.

Being Irish means . . .

some punches directed at you
are legacies from past generations.

Being Irish means . . .

your sister will punch *you* because
your brother punched *her*.

Being Irish means . . .

when people saw your entire
family in one place, your mother
was dubbed "a saint."

Being Irish means . . .

if you could reach it,
you could drink it.

Being Irish means . . .

you have way
too many hormones.

Being Irish means . . .

you "lost it" early.

Being Irish means . . .

you "found it" later.

Being Irish means . . .

you can "do it" a lot.

Being Irish means . . .

you've been "walked in on."

Being Irish means . . .

many of your sisters are Catherine,
Elizabeth, or Mary . . . and one is
Mary Catherine Elizabeth.

Being Irish means . . .

your fantasy life is very full.

Being Irish means . . .

your standards are very high,
but you're not slavishly
attached to them.

Being Irish means . . .

you're an easy touch.

Being Irish means . . .

someone in your family
is incredibly cheap.

Being Irish means . . .

it's more than likely you.

Being Irish means . . .

your beer can't be too cold,
too cheap, or too frequent.

Being Irish means . . .

you drink to forget,
but you forgot what
you're drinking to forget.

Being Irish means . . .

you don't know the words,
but that doesn't stop you
from singing.

Being Irish means . . .

"Irish stew" is the euphemism for
"boiled leftovers from the fridge."

Being Irish means . . .

you can't wait for the
other guy to stop talking
so you can start talking.

Being Irish means . . .

your stories get so long
that you forget the point.

Being Irish means . . .

the shortest duration of measurable
time in the history of mankind
is how long it takes your dad
to lose his temper.

Being Irish means . . .

as an Irishwoman, you are
an expert at doing two things
at once . . . and one of them is sex.

Being Irish means . . .

he might be lousy in bed,
but at least he's quick about it.

Being Irish means . . .

he might be lousy in bed,
but he seems to keep trying.

Being Irish means . . .

he might be lousy in bed,
but it doesn't slow him down.

Being Irish means . . .

you can talk her into it.

Being Irish means . . .

she actually doesn't mind
if you leave the TV on
(it gives her something to do).

Being Irish means . . .

at the exact moment you finish,
you're thinking about
the next time.

Being Irish means . . .

you don't need
fertility supplements.

Being Irish means . . .

if you're an Irishman,
you're a human sperm bank.

Being Irish means . . .

you appreciate quality,
but you prefer quantity.

Being Irish means . . .

your brother, as a joke,
runs naked through the party . . .
and no one notices.

Being Irish means . . .

you're not nearly as funny
as you think you are, but what
you lack in talent, you make up for
in frequency.

Being Irish means . . .

you've punched someone much
taller than you . . . of both sexes.

Being Irish means . . .

you're confused by all this
"modern technology," like
answering machines and VCRs.

Being Irish means . . .

"cheaper by the dozen"
refers specifically to your family.

Being Irish means . . .

your parents had it much
rougher than you . . . and they'll
never let you forget it.

Being Irish means . . .

you've had it much tougher
than your kids . . . and they have
no idea how tough it was.

Being Irish means . . .

your children are the punishment
for how much you tortured
your parents.

Being Irish means . . .

your grandparents seem
to snicker a lot.

Being Irish means . . .

someone in your family
was left behind at a party.

Being Irish means . . .

you have had "the spins"
in the last year.

Being Irish means . . .

you used to get embarrassed
when you were younger—
not so much anymore.

Being Irish means . . .

puberty resembled scenes from
The Exorcist.

Being Irish means . . .

you've made waaaay too many
promises to The Big Guy.

Being Irish means . . .

you fix the plumbing, woodworking,
and landscaping mistakes your
husband made when he was trying
to fix them in the first place.

Being Irish means . . .

there are sometimes people
at your kitchen table who you've
never seen before.

Being Irish means . . .

there wasn't a huge difference
between your last wake
and your last kegger party.

Being Irish means . . .

you have broken at least one bone
in your body without knowing or
remembering how you broke it.

Being Irish means . . .

you've been occasionally surprised
at the tensile strength
of your own skull.

Being Irish means . . .

you remember great jokes
at very bad times.

Being Irish means . . .

you've got a lot of explaining
to do at the Pearly Gates.

Being Irish means . . .

you've fallen fast asleep during
one of *your own* stories.

Being Irish means . . .

most of your very large
male relatives were called "Tiny"
"Shorty," or "Sir."

Being Irish means . . .

you are, or know someone,
named "Murph."

Being Irish means . . .

if you don't know Murph,
then you know Mac.

Being Irish means . . .

if you don't know Murph or Mac,
then you know Sully.

Being Irish means . . .

you probably also know
Sully McMurphy.

Being Irish means . . .

your family's crest has a
shot glass and a beer mug
somewhere in it.

Being Irish means . . .

one of your relatives
owns a tavern.

Being Irish means . . .

one of your relatives
is in construction.

Being Irish means . . .

one of your relatives
is in real estate.

Being Irish means . . .

one of your relatives is either
insane or a genius or both.

Being Irish means . . .

they're all overly nice
to the relative who's in
the city council.

Being Irish means . . .

your family tree has
several major weeds near it.

Being Irish means . . .

you have one aunt or uncle
who buries cash somewhere
in their backyard.

Being Irish means . . .

no matter what you do, two days
after any haircut your hair
looks exactly the same as always.

Being Irish means . . .

for no apparent rhyme
or reason, you have less hair
is some spots and more in others.

Being Irish means . . .

you're not a great liar, but you're
an incredible exaggerator,
fabricator, and omitter.

Being Irish means . . .

you saved up for that "rainy day"
but got a monsoon instead.

Being Irish means . . .

you love gardens . . . except
when you're waking up in one.

Being Irish means . . .

you stop to smell the roses,
but then accidentally
barf into them.

Being Irish means . . .

your parents were on a first-name
basis with everyone at the
local emergency room.

Being Irish means . . .

one sibling talked you into
doing something that even now
seems incredibly stupid—
but you did it anyway.

Being Irish means . . .

you are genetically incapable
of keeping a secret.

Being Irish means . . .

every secret you ever had
was broadcast that very same day
at the family dinner table.

Being Irish means . . .

your attention span is so short
that—oh, forget it.